KIDS CAN COOK

Fun and yummy recipes for budding chefs

Button
BOOKS

Illustrated by Esther Coombs

CONTENTS

3 **Before you begin**

4 **Equipment**

5 **Basic techniques**

Breakfasts, snacks & breads

8 **Scrambled eggs on toast**

9 **Fruit smoothies**

10 **Pancakes**

12 **Muffins**

14 **Sausage rolls**

15 **Corn quesadilla**

16 **Easy-bake bread**

18 **Cheese straws**

20 **Flatbread**

22 **Skewers**

24 **Banana bread**

26 **Mini frittatas**

Main meals & sauces

28 **Pasta sauces**

30 **Meatballs**

32 **Pizza**

34 **Pasta bake**

36 **Spaghetti bolognese**

38 **Risotto**

40 **Baked potatoes**

42 **Sliders**

44 **Chicken fajitas**

46 **Fishcakes**

48 **Curry**

Sweet treats

50 **Ice pops**

51 **Strawberry sundae**

52 **Apple pie**

53 **Oatmeal bars**

54 **Cupcakes**

56 **Cookies**

58 **Chocolate crispy treats**

59 **Vanilla fudge**

60 **Gingerbread people**

62 **Chocolate brownies**

BEFORE YOU BEGIN

Get ready to have lots of fun in the kitchen learning basic cooking skills and making delicious things for you, your family, and friends to eat!

Before you start, read through the recipe first to make sure you've got all the ingredients and equipment, and that you understand what you'll be doing. If you need to prepare any ingredients (such as peeling or chopping), do this before you start to cook. And never start cooking without the help of an adult!

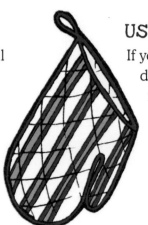

Using an oven/microwave oven

If you need to move any of the oven shelves, do this before turning it on. Cook food on the middle shelf of the oven unless the recipe says otherwise. Always wear oven mitts when taking anything out of a microwave or oven.

STAYING SAFE

* Make sure there's an adult there to help you.

* Always wash your hands before you start cooking, and when you've finished. Wash them after handling raw meat or fish, too.

* If you're wearing rings, take them off.

* Tie back long hair and wear an apron.

* Be very careful when using a sharp knife or a vegetable peeler.

* Never leave the kitchen when the stove is on.

* Use oven mitts when handling anything hot, and put hot dishes onto a trivet or heatproof mat.

* Turn pot handles to the side of the stove to keep them safely out of the way.

EQUIPMENT

Here are some really useful things to have in your kitchen. You'll also need measuring cups and spoons, cookware, and bakeware.

Pastry brush

Spatula

Measuring pitcher

Blender

Kitchen scale

Whisk

Strainer

Large mixing bowl

Garlic press

Oven mitts

Box grater

Kitchen scissors

Wooden spoon

Vegetable peeler

Rolling pin

Cutting board

Sharp knife

Citrus squeezer

BASIC TECHNIQUES

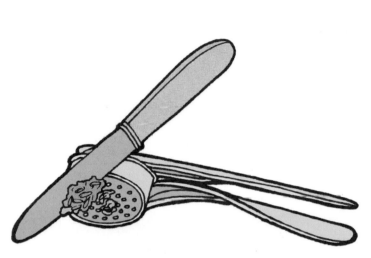

How to mince garlic

Cut the ends off a clove of garlic and peel it. Put it inside a garlic press and squeeze the handles together tightly. Use a knife to scrape off any garlic that is still sticking to the garlic press.

How to seed a bell pepper

Cut the top off a bell pepper. You will see the core and seeds inside. Use a sharp knife to cut away the parts attached to the bell pepper and pull away.

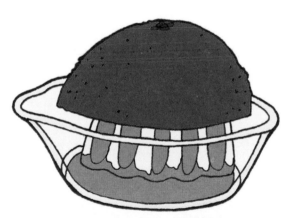

How to squeeze citrus fruits

Cut the orange (or you may be using a lemon or lime) in half. Put the half orange upside down on a squeezer and push down and twist to squeeze the juice out.

How to use a box grater

Place the grater on a cutting board and hold it firmly by the handle. Hold the cheese (or vegetable) in the other hand and rub up and down the grater. Be very careful that you don't catch your fingers or knuckles on the grater!

To zest citrus fruit, rub the brightly colored skin on the side that has little star shapes.

How to chop an onion

Put the onion on a cutting board and cut off the top. Cut in half through the root and remove the papery outer skin. Place one half of the onion flat side down and hold it firmly with the root pointing toward your little finger. Cut across the onion to make slices and discard the end with the root. To make the onion slices into dice, cut the other way across the onion.

How to crack an egg

Hold the egg in one hand, over a cup or bowl. Tap the middle of the egg with a knife to crack it. Push your thumbs into the crack and pull apart. Let the insides fall into the bowl. It's best to crack eggs into a separate bowl before adding to your recipe in case bits of the shell fall in there too!

How to beat an egg

Put your bowl on top of a damp cloth to stop it moving around. Beat the egg with a fork or whisk until it's frothy.

How to beat a mixture

Put your bowl on top of a damp cloth to stop it moving around. Use a wooden spoon to quickly stir the ingredients together until they are smooth and creamy.

How to sift flour

You need to sift flour to get rid of any large lumps. Put a strainer over a large bowl and spoon in the flour. Lift the strainer slightly and shake it from side to side. You may need to use a spoon to rub any large bits of flour through the strainer.

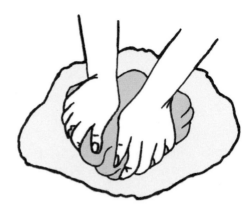

How to knead dough

Sprinkle a little flour onto your counter and use the heels of your hands to push the dough away from you. Then fold the dough in half, turn it around, and push away from you again. Keep on folding, turning, and pushing until it's smooth and stretchy (this takes about 5 to 10 minutes).

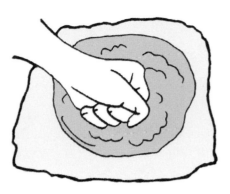

How to knock back dough

Punch down firmly with your fists and the dough will deflate.

How to roll out dough

Sprinkle a little flour onto your counter and rolling pin. Press down with the rolling pin and roll across the top of the dough, away from you. Rotate the dough and sprinkle more flour if needed. Keep rolling and rotating until the dough is the shape and thickness you want it.

How to see if a cake is cooked

Insert a skewer into the center of a cake. If it comes out clean, it's cooked. If there's batter on the skewer, put the cake back in the oven and bake for a few more minutes before testing again.

SCRAMBLED EGGS ON TOAST

Ingredients

2 eggs
1 tablespoon milk (optional)
1 teaspoon unsalted butter
1 slice of bread
butter, for spreading
salt and pepper

SERVES 1

1 Crack the eggs into a bowl. Add the milk (if using), season with a little salt and pepper, and beat together.

2 Melt the unsalted butter in a small nonstick saucepan over low to medium heat until it's frothy. Pour the egg mixture into the pan and pop the bread in the toaster. Cook the eggs for 2 to 3 minutes, or until just set, stirring occasionally with a wooden spoon and bringing the mixture in from the sides.

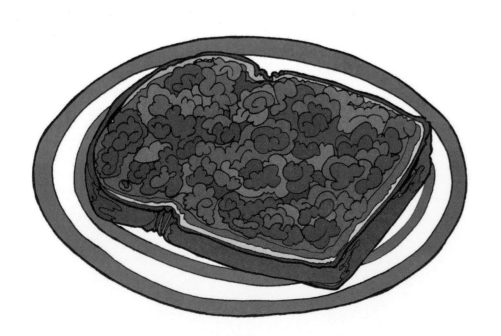

3 Spread the toast with a little butter, then spoon the scrambled eggs on top.

FRUIT SMOOTHIES

Ingredients

(FOR EACH SMOOTHIE)
1 ripe banana, sliced
1 to 2 teaspoons honey
    (optional)
$2/3$ cup lowfat milk,
    or dairy-free alternative
3 tablespoons plain yogurt,
    or dairy-free alternative
crushed ice

SUPER BERRY SMOOTHIE
$1^2/3$ cups berries, fresh or
    frozen (e.g. blueberries,
    raspberries, strawberries,
    or blackberries)

GORGEOUS GREEN SMOOTHIE
2 kiwifruit, peeled and
    chopped, or $2/3$ cup green
    grapes
$1/2$ apple, peeled, cored, and
    chopped
1 cup fresh spinach leaves

OUTRAGEOUS ORANGE SMOOTHIE
1 mango, peeled and sliced
$1/2$ melon, peeled and chopped
$2/3$ cup orange juice instead
    of the milk

SERVES 2

1 Put all the main ingredients
listed for a smoothie into a
blender and add the ingredients
of your choice of smoothie.
Whiz until smooth. If too thick,
add a little more milk or water.

ENGLISH PANCAKES

Ingredients

1 cup all-purpose flour
pinch of salt
2 eggs
³/₄ cup milk, topped off with
    5 tablespoons water
unsalted butter, for frying

TO SERVE
lemon wedges
superfine sugar

MAKES 8 to 10

1 Sift the flour and salt into a large mixing bowl. Use a spoon to make a hollow in the flour.

2 Crack the eggs (see page 6) and pour them into the hollow. Gently whisk them into the flour then add the milk, a little at a time, whisking until the batter is smooth.

3 Heat a little butter in a nonstick skillet over medium heat. Take off the heat and wipe away any excess butter with a piece of paper towel.

4 Put back over the heat and pour about half a ladle of batter into the pan. Tilt the pan in all directions so that a thin layer of batter covers the bottom.

5 Cook the pancake for a minute or so until it starts to bubble and turn golden. Turn over with a spatula or palette knife then cook the other side. Slide out of the pan onto a warm plate.

6 Sprinkle with lemon juice and sugar, and fold in half and half again to form a triangle or roll it. Make more pancakes until all the batter is used up, adding more butter for frying as necessary.

PANCAKES

Ingredients

1 cup all-purpose flour
1 teapoon baking powder
$\frac{1}{2}$ teaspoon baking soda
2 tablespoons superfine
    sugar
pinch of salt
1 egg
$\frac{2}{3}$ cup milk
unsalted butter, for frying

TO SERVE
Maple syrup (or honey)
Toppings of your choice, such
    as: fresh fruit, cooked
    lean bacon, peanut butter,
    crème fraîche, or ice cream

MAKES 8 to 10

1 Sift together the flour, baking powder, baking soda, sugar, and salt into a large bowl. Heat the oven to 225°F. Then follow steps 2 to 3 of the pancake recipe on the opposite page to make the batter and grease the skillet.

2 Put the pan back over the heat and use a ladle to pour dollops of batter into the pan—make sure they're not too close because they'll spread when cooking. Don't tilt the pan after you've added the batter! Cook for about 2 minutes until the pancakes look golden and firm, then flip over and cook the other side.

3 Remove from the pan, transfer to a baking sheet, and put into the oven to keep warm while you make the rest of the pancakes. Serve stacked up on a plate with a drizzle of maple syrup and any of your favorite toppings.

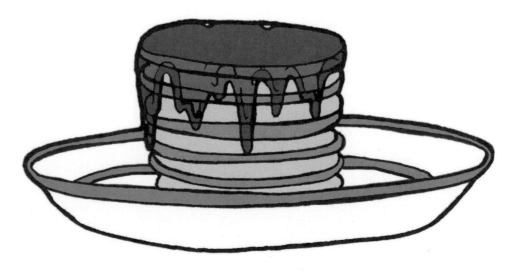

MUFFINS

Try out different combinations of fruit or chocolate in these simple muffin recipes. For light, fluffy muffins, the trick is not to overmix the batter: just gently stir your ingredients to combine.

Tip

Muffins are best eaten on the day they're made, or you can freeze them to have another time. They'll keep for 2 to 3 days in an airtight container lined with paper towel.

BLUEBERRY MUFFINS

Ingredients

1 egg
3 tablespoons vegetable oil
$3/4$ cup buttermilk
2 cups all-purpose flour
2 teaspoons baking powder
$1/2$ teaspoon baking soda
$1/2$ cup superfine sugar, plus extra for sprinkling
pinch of salt
$1\frac{1}{4}$ cups blueberries (if frozen, don't thaw before cooking!)

MAKES 12

1 Heat the oven to 375°F. Line a 12-cup muffin pan with paper liners (use 9 paper liners for larger muffins, 12 for smaller ones).

2 In a pitcher, whisk together the egg, oil, and buttermilk.

3 Sift the flour, baking powder, baking soda, sugar, and salt into a large bowl. Carefully stir in the buttermilk mixture with a wooden spoon until just combined. It doesn't matter if there are still lumps in it. Gently fold in the blueberries until just evenly distributed, setting aside a handful for later.

4 Divide the batter between the muffin liners and dot the reserved blueberries on top. Sprinkle with sugar. Bake for 20 to 25 minutes or until risen and golden, and test one with a skewer (see page 7). Leave in the pan for 5 minutes, then transfer to a wire rack to cool completely.

CHOCOLATE CHIP MUFFINS

Ingredients

2¹/₂ cups all-purpose flour
1 tablespoon baking powder
¹/₂ teaspoon baking soda
2 tablespoons unsweetened
   cocoa powder
¹/₄ teaspoon salt
¹/₂ cup superfine sugar
1 egg
2 tablespoons sunflower oil
³/₄ cup milk
³/₄ cup chocolate chips
   (semisweet, milk, or white)

MAKES 12

1 Heat the oven to 400°F. Line a 12-cup muffin pan with paper liners.

2 Sift the flour, baking powder, baking soda, cocoa powder, and salt into a large bowl, then stir in the sugar.

3 In a pitcher, whisk together the egg, oil, and milk.

4 Make a hollow in the center of the flour then carefully stir in the milk mixture until just combined. It doesn't matter if there are still lumps in it. Fold in the chocolate chips until just evenly distributed, setting aside a handful for later.

5 Spoon the batter into the muffin liners and dot the reserved chocolate chips on top. Bake for 20 to 25 minutes or until risen and golden, and test one with a skewer (see page 7). Leave in the pan for 5 minutes, then transfer to a wire rack to cool completely.

SAUSAGE ROLLS

Ingredients

1 x 11¼-ounce package ready-
   roll puff pastry
6 good-quality sausages
1 small onion, very finely
   chopped (optional)
6 sage leaves, finely chopped,
   or 1 teaspoon dried
   (optional)
flour, for dusting
1 egg, beaten

MAKES 8 to 16

Tip

Try out some other herbs.
Parsley and thyme are good too!

1 Heat the oven to 425°F.
Line a baking sheet with
parchment paper.

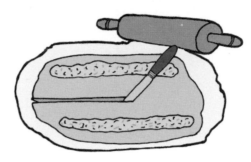

3 Unroll the pastry on a lightly
floured counter and cut in half
lengthwise. Spread the meat in
a long sausage shape along the
length of the pastry, slightly
off center.

2 Snip the ends off the sausages
and squeeze the meat into a bowl.
Add the onion and sage (if using)
and mix well with your hands.
Divide the meat mixture into
2 pieces.

4 Brush one long edge of pastry
with beaten egg and roll up
tightly from the other side. Press
down to secure. Cut into pieces
and place on the baking sheet.

5 Carefully make 2 slashes in
the top of each piece and brush
with beaten egg. Bake in the
oven for 20 to 25 minutes or until
puffed up, golden, and crisp.

CORN QUESADILLA

Ingredients

1/4 cup grated cheddar cheese
1 flour tortilla
a few strips of leftover
  chicken or cooked
  vegetables such as
  mushrooms, onions, or
  red bell peppers (optional)
1 tablespoon corn
1/2 teaspoon chopped fresh
  cilantro
oil, for brushing

SERVES 1

1 Sprinkle the cheese over one half of the tortilla, leaving a border around the edge. Sprinkle over the leftover chicken or vegetables (if using) and top with the corn and cilantro.

Tip

Flour tortillas are easier to fold than corn ones and hold more ingredients, but you still need to be careful not to overfill them!

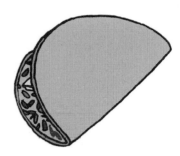

2 Fold over the other half of the tortilla so you have a half-moon shape.

3 Brush a nonstick skillet with oil and heat over low to medium heat. When the pan is hot, use a spatula to place the quesadilla in the pan and cook for about 2 minutes on each side or until it is crisp and golden. Cut into wedges and serve.

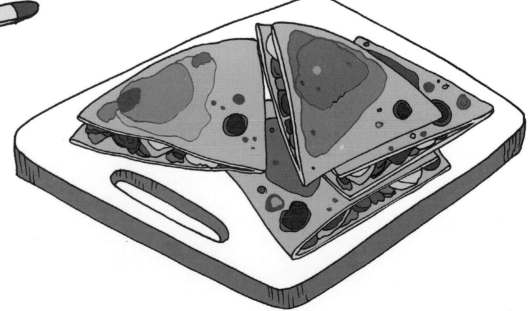

EASY-BAKE BREAD

Ingredients

2½ cups strong white
   bread flour, plus extra
   for kneading
½ teaspoon salt
1 teaspoon superfine sugar
1 teaspoon dried yeast
¾ cup warm water
1 tablespoon olive oil, plus
   extra for oiling

MAKES 1

Variation

Brush the top with beaten
egg and sprinkle over some
sunflower seeds before baking.

How to store
fresh bread

Store uncovered at room
temperature for the first day,
then wrap in a paper bag for
the next day. If freezing, slice
the bread first.

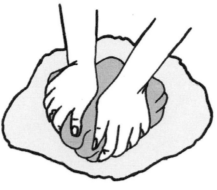

1 Sift the flour into a large bowl and stir in the salt, sugar, and yeast. Make a big hole in the center with a wooden spoon and pour in the warm water and the oil. Mix together with the spoon to form a soft dough.

2 Dust your hands and counter with flour. Tip the dough out onto the counter. Knead the dough by pushing it away from you and then folding it in half and pushing it again and again for about 5 minutes until it's smooth and stretchy.

3 Wash and dry your bowl, then rub the inside with a little oil. Pop the dough back into the bowl and cover with a clean dish towel. Leave in a warm place for about an hour until the dough has doubled in size.

Tip

Don't add too much flour. A wet dough is better than a dry one, which will be tough when baked.

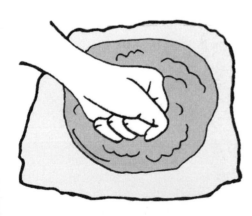

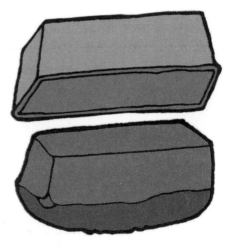

4 Punch down with your fists to knock back the dough. Place on a lightly floured counter and knead for another 5 minutes.

5 Shape the dough into a rectangle and place in a lightly oiled 2-pound loaf pan. Cover and leave in a warm place for about an hour until it has doubled in size. Then heat the oven to 425°F.

6 Bake on the middle shelf of the oven for 30 to 35 minutes until golden. Tip out of the pan and tap the base—it should sound hollow when fully cooked. If not cooked, put the loaf back in the oven and test again after 10 minutes. When cooked, turn out onto a wire rack and let cool.

CHEESE STRAWS

Ingredients

2 cups all-purpose flour, plus extra
   for dusting
pinch of salt
$2/3$ cup ($1 1/3$ sticks) cold unsalted butter,
   cut into cubes
$3/4$ cup grated Parmesan cheese,
   plus extra for sprinkling
1 egg, beaten
cold water, to mix

MAKES ABOUT 24

Tip

You can use gluten-free
flour instead of all-purpose flour.
Your cheese straws will still
taste just as good!

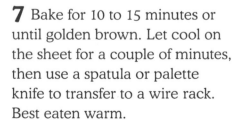

1 Line a baking sheet with parchment paper and set aside.

2 Sift the flour into a large bowl and add the salt and butter.

3 Using your fingertips, rub the butter into the flour until all the lumps are gone and the mixture looks like fine bread crumbs. Stir in the grated cheese.

4 Add half the beaten egg and mix with a knife. Add a little cold water (about 1 to 2 tablespoons) to form a stiff dough, using your hands to bring it together into a ball. If it's too dry, add a little more water. If it's too wet, add a little more flour. Wrap in plastic wrap and chill for 30 minutes.

5 Heat the oven to 375°F. Dust a clean counter with flour and roll out the dough into a rectangle about ⅛ inch thick (see page 7). Brush with the remaining beaten egg if you have enough, or some milk, and sprinkle with cheese.

6 Cut into ½-inch strips using a pizza wheel or knife. Cut each strip into 2 or 3 pieces and place on the baking sheet.

Variations

Try adding half a teaspoon of one of the following at the end of step 2: mustard powder, cayenne pepper, paprika, finely chopped basil, or yeast extract.

7 Bake for 10 to 15 minutes or until golden brown. Let cool on the sheet for a couple of minutes, then use a spatula or palette knife to transfer to a wire rack. Best eaten warm.

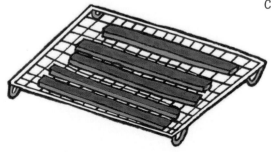

FLATBREAD

Ingredients

1²/₃ cups self-rising flour,
   plus extra for dusting
¹/₂ teaspoon baking powder
¹/₄ teaspoon salt
²/₃ cup plain yogurt
warm water, to mix
olive oil, for frying

MAKES 4

1 Place all the ingredients (except the olive oil) in a large bowl and mix together with a wooden spoon. Use your hands to bring them together into a ball, adding a little water if necessary.

2 Knead the dough in the bowl for about a minute (see page 7). If the dough's too sticky, add a little more flour. If it's too dry, add a little more water.

Variations

Try adding one of the following in step 1: half a bunch of finely chopped fresh herbs such as flat-leaf parsley, cilantro, or basil; a teaspoon of dried mint or a clove of minced garlic.

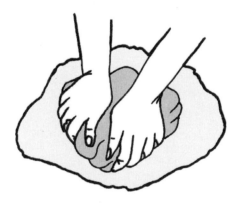

3 Dust a clean counter with flour and tip the dough out onto it. Knead for a minute or so by pushing it away from you and then folding it in half and pushing it again and again.

4 Divide the dough into 4 equal parts then roll each piece out into teardrop shapes or circles about ¹/₈ inch thick (see page 7).

Tip

Clean doughy hands by dusting them with a little more flour and then rubbing them over another bowl or the trash can.

How to eat flatbread

* Use as a base for an
  open sandwich *

* Top with a thin layer of
tomato sauce, sliced veggies, and
cheese, and pop under a broiler
for 5 minutes *

* Have as a side dish for a curry
(see page 48) *

* Dip into hummus or
a minty yogurt dip *

5 Brush a skillet with a little oil
and heat over medium to high
heat. When the pan is hot, cook
the flatbread over high heat for 1
to 2 minutes on each side until it
is puffed up, with a few spots of
brown. Turn it over with tongs.

6 Keep the flatbread warm by
wrapping in foil or a dish towel
until the rest are cooked.

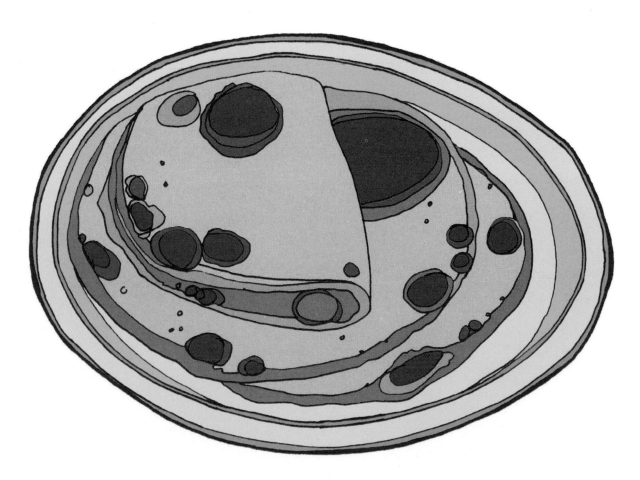

SKEWERS

You can mix and match all kinds of vegetables, meat, and fish on skewers. They're quick and easy to cook, too! The method is the same for all the recipes here. Just put the main ingredient in the marinade, then follow the steps for halloumi skewers. If using wooden skewers, soak them in water for 30 minutes first to stop them burning.

HALLOUMI SKEWERS

Ingredients

1 package halloumi, cut
   into chunks
1 zucchini, cut into
   thick slices
1 red onion, cut into
   wedges and separated
8 cherry tomatoes

FOR THE MARINADE
juice of 1 lemon
4 tablespoons olive oil
1 garlic clove, minced
pinch of dried oregano
salt and pepper

MAKES 8 SKEWERS

1 Put all the ingredients for the marinade into a bowl and mix together. Add the halloumi and let marinate for 30 minutes.

2 Take the halloumi out of the marinade and thread onto skewers, alternating with the vegetables. Watch out for the sharp ends.

3 Put the skewers under the broiler. Cook for 10 to 12 minutes, turning once and basting with the marinade.

PORK AND PINEAPPLE SKEWERS

Ingredients

7 ounces pork tenderloin, cut into chunks

1 small can pineapple, drained and cut into chunks

1 green bell pepper, seeded and cut into chunks

1 onion, cut into wedges and separated

FOR THE MARINADE
juice of 1 lime
2 tablespoons olive oil
2 tablespoons cider vinegar
1 tablespoon brown sugar

CHICKEN SKEWERS

Ingredients

2 chicken breasts, cut into chunks

FOR THE MARINADE
2 tablespoons olive oil
1 garlic clove, minced
juice of $\frac{1}{2}$ lemon
1 tablespoon soy sauce
1 tablespoon runny honey

TOFU SKEWERS

Ingredients

1 package smoked tofu, cut into chunks

1 zucchini, cut into thick slices

1 red bell pepper, seeded and cut into chunks

16 button mushrooms

FOR THE MARINADE
2 tablespoons tomato paste
2 tablespoons soy sauce
juice of $\frac{1}{2}$ lemon
1 tablespoon olive oil
1 tablespoon runny honey

BANANA BREAD

Ingredients

½ cup (1 stick) unsalted butter, plus extra for greasing
⅜ cup soft light brown sugar
2 eggs
1 teaspoon vanilla extract
3 ripe bananas
½ cup walnuts, coarsely chopped, or chocolate chips (optional)
1⅓ cups self-rising flour
1 teaspoon baking powder
pinch of salt

SERVES 8 to 10

Tip

For a gluten-free loaf, replace the flour with rice flour and ½ teaspoon xanthan gum.

1 Place the butter in a glass bowl and microwave on high in short bursts, or melt in a saucepan over low heat.

2 Heat the oven to 325°F. Pour the melted butter into a large bowl. Add the sugar and beat together with a wooden spoon.

3 Crack the eggs into a separate bowl (see page 6) then stir into the butter mixture until well mixed. Stir in the vanilla extract.

4 In another bowl, mash the bananas with a fork (they don't have to be completely smooth).

5 Stir the mashed bananas into the mixture. Stir in the chopped walnuts or chocolate chips (if using).

6 Sift the flour, baking powder, and salt into another bowl.

7 Add the flour mixture to the banana batter about a quarter at a time, stirring with a wooden spoon after each addition.

8 Grease a 2-pound loaf pan and line with parchment paper. Pour in the banana bread batter and gently shake the pan from side to side to help the batter settle.

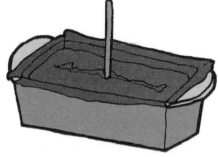

9 Bake in the oven on the middle shelf for about 45 minutes, or until a skewer comes out clean (see page 7). Let cool in the pan for 10 minutes before transferring to a wire rack.

Tip

Banana bread stays fresh for up to 4 days in an airtight container or can be frozen.

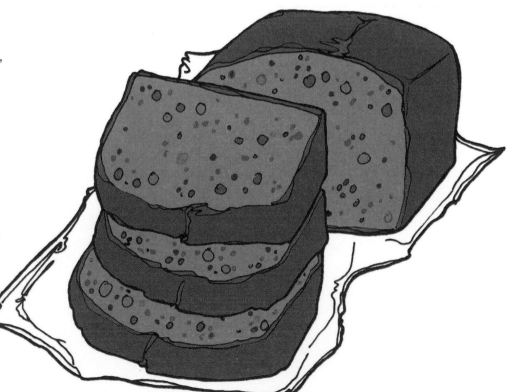

MINI FRITTATAS

Ingredients

1 tablespoon olive oil, plus extra for greasing
1 red onion, finely diced
1 red bell pepper, seeded and finely diced
2 cups baby leaf spinach, coarsely chopped
handful of basil leaves, torn into pieces
1/2 cup frozen peas
6 eggs
1/2 cup milk
3/4 cup grated cheddar cheese

MAKES 12

1 Heat the oven to 400°F. Heat the oil in a skillet over medium heat and gently fry the onion and pepper for about 5 minutes or until softened.

2 Remove the pan from the heat and stir in the spinach and basil leaves. These will wilt in the heat. Then stir in the peas, too.

3 Crack the eggs into a bowl, add the milk, and whisk together. Stir in half the cheese.

4 Lightly grease a muffin pan with olive oil. Distribute the cooked vegetables between each muffin cup.

5 Pour or spoon the egg mixture evenly into the muffin cups until each is about three-quarters full and sprinkle the rest of the cheese on top. Bake in the oven for 20 to 25 minutes until golden brown and cooked through.

6 Check that the frittatas are cooked in the middle by poking one of the centers with a skewer or knife tip. If it hasn't set, put back in the oven to cook for a few more minutes.

Variations

You can use all kinds of vegetables and cheese in a frittata.
Why not try one of the following combinations?

SWEET POTATO & BLUE CHEESE
Replace the spinach, basil, peas, and cheese with the flesh of a baked sweet potato and some crumbled blue cheese.

MUSHROOM & SPINACH
Replace the red bell pepper, basil, and peas with $1/8$ cup finely sliced cremini mushrooms cooked in 2 tablespoons unsalted butter for 10 minutes.

BACON & GOAT CHEESE
Chop 4 slices of bacon into small pieces and fry along with the red onion and bell pepper in step 1 until the bacon is brown and crisp. Use goat cheese instead of cheddar and leave out the spinach, basil, and peas.

PASTA SAUCES

These three easy sauces are packed with goodness and can be stirred through all kinds of cooked pasta, from twists to tagliatelle. Each sauce is enough for four people when served with pasta. The tomato sauce can also be used as a pizza topping.

TOMATO SAUCE

Ingredients
1 tablespoon olive oil
1 small onion, finely chopped
1 garlic clove, minced
1 tablespoon tomato paste
1 x 14-ounce can chopped tomatoes
pinch of sugar (optional)
handful of fresh basil leaves, torn into small pieces
salt and pepper

1 Heat the oil in a saucepan over low heat, then add the onion and garlic and gently fry for about 5 minutes, until softened and pale gold.

2 Add the tomato paste and tomatoes to the pan. Half-fill the can with water, add to the pan, and stir. Turn the heat up to bring to a boil, then turn down again until it is gently bubbling (simmering). Cook for 10 to 15 minutes until the sauce thickens, stirring occasionally.

3 Season with salt and pepper and add a pinch of sugar if it tastes a little bitter. Stir in the torn basil leaves.

CHEESE SAUCE

Ingredients

3 tablespoons butter
3 tablespoons all-
purpose flour
2½ cups milk

1 cup grated cheddar
cheese
salt and pepper

1 Melt the butter in a pan over low heat. Stir in the flour and cook for 1 to 2 minutes.

2 Stir in the milk, a little at a time, to get a smooth sauce. Bring to a boil, stirring all the time, then turn down the heat until it is gently bubbling and cook until the sauce thickens.

3 Turn off the heat. Stir in the cheese to melt it and season with salt and pepper.

PESTO

Ingredients

⅓ cup pine nuts
½ garlic clove
pinch of salt
large bunch of basil
½ cup grated Parmesan
cheese
juice of ½ lemon
¼ cup extra virgin olive oil

Vegan variation

Replace the cheese with 3 tablespoons nutritional yeast flakes and a pinch of salt.

1 Put the pine nuts, garlic, salt, and basil into a small food processor or blender and whiz together until coarsely chopped.

2 Transfer to a bowl and stir in the cheese and lemon juice. Stir in the olive oil—you need just enough to bind all the ingredients together, so you might not use all of it.

MEATBALLS

Ingredients

1 pound lean ground meat (e.g. beef, pork, turkey, veal, or half beef/half pork)
1 teaspoon salt
3 slices of bread, crusts removed
2 garlic cloves, minced
1 small onion, finely chopped
2 tablespoons chopped flat-leaf parsley
1 egg
1 teaspoon Worcestershire sauce or soy sauce
2 x quantity Tomato Sauce (see page 28)

TO SERVE
cooked pasta, rice, or crusty bread
grated Parmesan cheese

MAKES ABOUT 20 MEDIUM OR 40 SMALL MEATBALLS

1 Put the meat and the salt in a large bowl, and break up the meat with a fork.

2 Tear the bread into pieces and put in a food processor or blender. Whiz to make small bread crumbs.

3 Add the rest of the meatball ingredients, including the bread crumbs, to the bowl. Mix everything together using clean hands.

4 Roll the mixture into balls. This is easier if you dampen your hands with a little water first.

5 Heat the oven to 400°F. Line a baking sheet with parchment paper and spread out the meatballs. Cook for about 15 to 20 minutes until browned, turning over halfway through cooking. Bigger meatballs take longer to cook!

6 While the meatballs are cooking, make the tomato sauce (see page 28).

7 Transfer the meatballs to a plate lined with paper towel to soak up any grease.

8 Carefully place the meatballs into the tomato sauce to keep warm. Sprinkle with grated cheese and serve with crusty bread or spooned over cooked spaghetti or rice.

Tip

Freeze any leftover meatballs and sauce in a suitable container.

Other ways to eat meatballs

Meatballs don't have to be cooked in a tomato sauce! Try the following options:

* Simmer in a spicy soup *

* Slide into a sub-style sandwich, or pop into a pita pocket with salad greens and a minty yogurt dressing *

* Serve Swedish-style in a thick gravy with mashed potato *

PIZZA

Ingredients

3 cups strong white bread flour,
    plus extra for kneading
$1/2$ teaspoon salt
1 teaspoon superfine sugar
1 teaspoon dried yeast
$3/4$ cup warm water
1 tablespoon olive oil, plus extra
    for oiling and drizzling
pizza sauce or strained tomatoes
$1/2$ cup grated cheddar cheese
1 ball of mozzarella, torn into pieces
basil leaves, torn
grated Parmesan cheese, for sprinkling

MAKES 2 LARGE OR 4 SMALL PIZZAS

Extra topping ideas

* Bell peppers * mushrooms * ham * pineapple *
* olives * corn * zucchini * tuna * onions *
anchovies * peeled shrimp *

1 Sift the flour into a large bowl and stir in the salt, sugar, and yeast. Make a big hole in the center with a wooden spoon and pour in the warm water and the oil. Mix together with the spoon to form a soft dough.

2 Dust your hands and counter with flour. Tip the dough out onto the counter. Knead the dough by pushing it away from you and then folding it in half and pushing it again and again for about 5 minutes until it's smooth and stretchy.

3 Wash and dry your bowl, then rub the inside with a little oil. Pop the dough back into the bowl and cover with a clean dish towel. Leave in a warm place for about an hour until the dough has doubled in size.

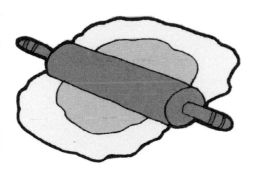

Variation

For a pepperoni pizza, in step 6, top the pizza with slices of pepperoni before adding the basil, grated Parmesan cheese, and a drizzle of olive oil.

4 Heat the oven to 475°F. Knead the dough again for 30 seconds, then cut it into 2 or 4 pieces. Roll each piece of dough out into thin circles about ¼ inch thick (see page 7). Place on 2 baking sheets greased with a little oil.

5 Spread the pizza sauce or strained tomatoes thinly over the bases using the back of a spoon but don't spread it on the edges, which will become the crusts.

6 Sprinkle the grated cheddar cheese, mozzarella, and basil all over your pizza bases. Top with a sprinkling of Parmesan cheese and drizzle with olive oil. Bake for 12 to 15 minutes until golden and bubbling.

PASTA BAKE

Ingredients

8 ounces dried pasta shells or twists
1 head of broccoli, broken into florets
1 leek, halved and sliced
1 x quantity Cheese Sauce (see page 29)
8 to 10 cherry tomatoes, halved
½ cup bread crumbs
¼ cup grated Parmesan cheese
salt and pepper

SERVES 4

How to make bread crumbs

Cut the crusts off a slice of bread (can be brown or white). Tear into pieces then put in a food processor or blender and whiz. You can make bread crumbs from several slices of bread and keep in the freezer until you need them. Each slice of bread will make about ¼ cup bread crumbs.

1 Cook the pasta in a large pan of salted boiling water according to the package directions.

2 Add the broccoli and leek for the final 4 minutes of cooking time. Drain well and return to the pan.

3 Make the cheese sauce (see page 29).

4 Stir the cheese sauce into the cooked pasta and vegetables and mix well. Season with a little salt and pepper.

5 Use a large spoon to transfer to an ovenproof dish and spread out evenly.

6 Sprinkle the cherry tomatoes on top, followed by the bread crumbs and grated cheese. Bake in the oven at 375°F for 20 to 25 minutes until the topping is golden brown and bubbling.

Variation

Substitute roasted vegetables for the broccoli and leek. Slice up zucchini, red onion, eggplant, and red bell pepper, and put in a roasting pan. Sprinkle with olive oil and shake the pan from side to side to lightly coat the vegetables in oil. Cook in the oven for about 45 minutes until tender, turning once or twice. Add to the drained pasta (see step 2) then continue with the rest of the recipe.

Tip

This will keep in the refrigerator for up to 3 days. To reheat, cover with foil and put in a moderate oven for 20 minutes.

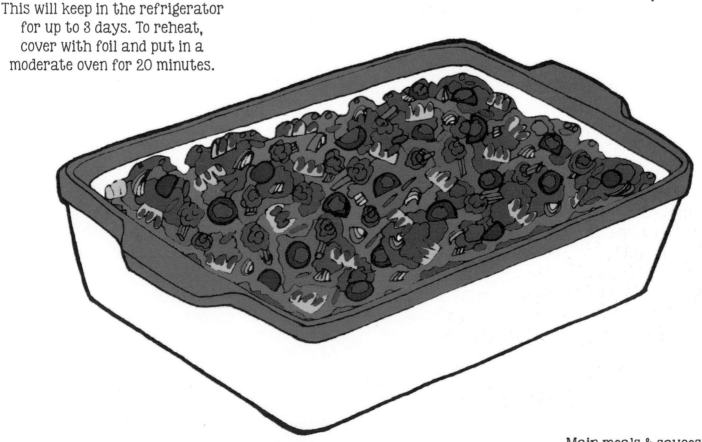

SPAGHETTI BOLOGNESE

Ingredients

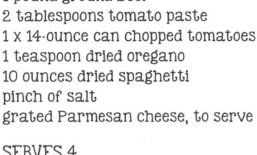

1 tablespoon olive oil
1 onion, finely chopped
2 garlic cloves, minced
1 carrot, finely chopped
1 celery stalk, finely chopped
1 pound ground beef
2 tablespoons tomato paste
1 x 14-ounce can chopped tomatoes
1 teaspoon dried oregano
10 ounces dried spaghetti
pinch of salt
grated Parmesan cheese, to serve

SERVES 4

Vegan variation

Replace the ground beef with 1 cup dried red lentils, 2 teaspoons soy sauce, and 2 cups vegetable stock. Leave out step 2. Add the lentils and stock in step 3, then cook for 15 to 20 minutes or until the lentils are just tender. Sprinkle with nutritional yeast flakes to serve.

Tips

* Add extra vegetables in step 1, such as 9 ounces chopped mushrooms, a sliced zucchini, or chopped red bell pepper *

* Stir in a bag of chopped spinach just before the end of cooking time *

1 Put a large saucepan on low heat and add the olive oil. Gently fry the onion, garlic, carrot, and celery stalk for 10 minutes, or until softened.

2 Increase the heat to medium to high and add the ground beef to the pan. Cook for about 5 minutes, stirring with a wooden spoon to break up the meat, or until it is browned all over.

3 Stir in the tomato paste then add the chopped tomatoes. Half-fill the tomato can with water, add to the pan, and stir. Stir in the dried oregano.

4 Bring to a boil, then reduce the heat so it is gently bubbling and cover with a lid. Cook over low heat for about 1 hour, removing the lid halfway through. Stir occasionally until you have a rich, thick sauce. If the sauce looks like drying out, add a little more water. Season with a little salt to taste.

5 Cook the spaghetti in a large pan of salted water according to the package directions. Drain. Divide the pasta between plates and top with spoonfuls of bolognese sauce and a sprinkling of grated cheese.

Other ways to use bolognese sauce

* Layer up with pasta sheets and cheese sauce (see page 29) to make lasagna *

* Makes a great filling for baked potatoes (see page 40) *

* Freeze leftover sauce to use at a later date *

RISOTTO

Ingredients

4 cups chicken or vegetable stock
1 tablespoon olive oil
3 tablespoons unsalted butter
1 red onion, finely chopped
1 garlic clove, minced
1½ cups risotto rice (carnaroli is the
  easiest to cook)
½ cup grated Parmesan cheese,
  plus extra to serve

SERVES 3 to 4

Tip

This is a great basic recipe and once you know how to make it you can add other ingredients. Fried bacon, cooked vegetables, and chopped herbs, for example, can go in at the end of step 5.

1 Pour the stock into a saucepan and bring up to a boil, then turn the heat down to a simmer (when it is gently bubbling).

2 Heat the olive oil and half the butter in a large saucepan over low heat. Add the onion and garlic and cook gently for about 10 to 15 minutes until really soft, stirring occasionally with a wooden spoon.

3 Increase the heat a little, add the rice to the pan, and stir to coat with the butter and oil. Cook for 1 minute.

4 Add 2 ladlefuls of the hot stock to the large saucepan and cook, stirring gently, until the liquid has been absorbed by the rice.

5 Keep adding the stock, 2 ladlefuls at a time and cook, still stirring, for about 20 minutes, until the rice is tender. Take a small spoon and taste the rice to see if it's cooked—it should be soft and creamy but with a slight "bite" to it.

6 Take the pan off the heat and stir in the rest of the butter and the cheese. Add a little extra grated cheese before serving.

Tip

If you run out of stock before the rice is cooked, add some boiling water.

BAKED POTATOES

Super-easy baked potatoes can be stuffed with any of your favorite fillings, from chili con carne to cheesy beans or tuna mayo. If you want to cut down on cooking time, once you've washed and pricked the potatoes, microwave on high for 5 minutes, then put in the oven for about 30 minutes to crisp up.

Tip
Yukon Gold and Russet potatoes are good for baking. You need a mealy type rather than a waxy potato.

SIMPLE BAKED POTATO

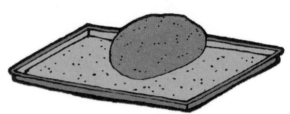

Ingredients
1 baking potato per person
sea salt
butter

1 Heat the oven to 400°F. Wash the potatoes and prick all over with a fork.

2 Roll each potato in a little salt and then place directly on the rack in the middle of the oven. Bake for 1 to 1½ hours or until soft in the center.

3 Put on a plate and don't open it until ready to eat. Hold one side with a dish towel and cut a cross in the top, then gently pull apart with a fork. Or put the dish towel on top of the potato and hit it with your fist! Dot with butter and sprinkle with salt.

CHEESY STUFFED BAKED POTATOES

Ingredients

2 baking potatoes
sea salt
2 teaspoons butter
2 tablespoons sour cream
2 scallions, finely chopped,
   or 2 teaspoons chopped chives
1/2 cup grated cheddar cheese

SERVES 2

1 Follow steps 1 to 2 of the recipe for the simple baked potato on page 40. Remove from the oven and cut in half. Scoop the potato flesh into a bowl. Add the butter, sour cream, scallions, and half the cheese and mix together with a fork. Season to taste with salt.

Variation

Stuff a sweet potato instead of a regular baking potato. It only takes about half the time to cook and is just as versatile.

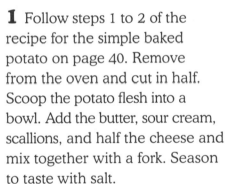

2 Spoon the mixture back into the potato skins and place on a baking sheet. Sprinkle over the remaining cheese and pop back in the oven for 10 to 15 minutes until the cheese has melted.

SLIDERS

Sliders are tiny burgers served in mini buns. You can swap the ground beef for lamb or turkey if desired. The veggie sliders recipe uses the same serving ingredients as the beef sliders and makes the same quantity.

BEEF SLIDERS

Ingredients
olive oil, for frying
1 red onion, finely chopped
2 slices of bread, crusts
   removed
8 ounces ground beef
¼ cup finely grated
   Parmesan cheese
1 egg
1 tablespoon tomato paste
½ teaspoon salt

TO SERVE
6 to 8 small burger buns
1 lettuce
2 tomatoes, sliced
cheese slices
toothpicks

MAKES 6 to 8

1 Add a little olive oil to a skillet and gently fry the onions over low heat for about 10 minutes or until soft. Put to one side to cool.

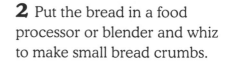

2 Put the bread in a food processor or blender and whiz to make small bread crumbs.

3 Put the ground beef in a bowl and break up with a fork.

4 Add the rest of the ingredients, including the bread crumbs, to the bowl. Mix everything together using clean hands.

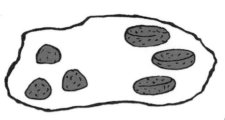

5 Divide into 6 to 8 equal-sized balls then press down to make patties about ¾ inch thick. Place on a plate and cover with plastic wrap. Chill in the refrigerator for at least 30 minutes to firm up so they're easier to cook.

6 Preheat the broiler to medium heat. Place the patties on a broiler rack and broil for 3 to 4 minutes on each side or until charred and thoroughly cooked.

7 Sandwich the sliders between the buns along with the toppings and secure with toothpicks.

VEGGIE SLIDERS

Ingredients

1 x 14-ounce can chickpeas, drained and rinsed
juice of ½ lemon, plus zest
small bunch of cilantro, leaves only
2 slices of bread, crusts removed,
    torn into pieces

½ cup chopped nuts (e.g. cashews, almonds)
1 carrot, grated
1 teaspoon ground cumin
1 egg
salt and pepper

1 Put all the ingredients into a food processor or blender and whiz together. Tip into a bowl then follow steps 5 to 7 above.

CHICKEN FAJITAS

Ingredients
2 chicken breasts, cut into strips
1 red onion, finely sliced
1 red and 1 yellow bell pepper, seeded
  and cut into thin strips
4 flour tortillas
lettuce leaves

FOR THE MARINADE
juice of 2 limes
1 teaspoon olive oil
3 teaspoons fajita seasoning mix,
  or 1 teaspoon each of dried oregano,
  ground cumin, and smoked paprika
1 garlic clove, minced

FOR THE GUACAMOLE
2 ripe avocados, halved and pitted
juice of 1 lime
2 tomatoes, coarsely chopped
2 teaspoons freshly chopped cilantro

SERVES 4

Tip
For meat-free fajitas, replace the chicken with
4 large flat mushrooms, thickly sliced.

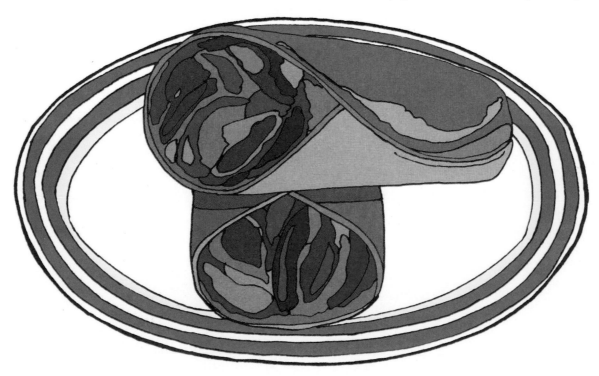

1 In a large bowl, add the lime juice, olive oil, fajita seasoning, and garlic and mix together to make the marinade.

2 Stir in the chicken, onion, and peppers and put to one side while you make the guacamole.

3 To make the guacamole, scoop out the avocado flesh into a bowl and mash with a fork. Stir in the lime juice, chopped tomatoes, and cilantro.

4 Heat the oven to 350°F. Wrap the tortillas in aluminum foil and place them on the middle shelf.

5 While the tortillas are warming through, heat a skillet and add the chicken, vegetables, and marinade to the pan. Cook over medium to high heat for about 10 minutes, stirring occasionally to prevent sticking on the bottom.

6 You can check if the chicken is cooked by cutting through a thick piece to look at the color. Carry on cooking the chicken if it is still pink inside.

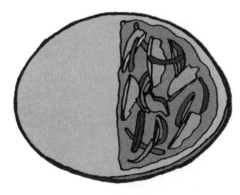 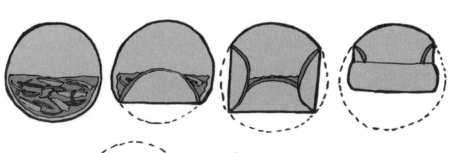

7 Spread the top middle half of each warmed tortilla with guacamole, leaving the other end and sides empty. Top with lettuce leaves and some of the chicken and vegetables, but don't add too much filling or you won't be able to fold the tortilla!

8 Fold the bottom up and over the lower edge of the filling, then overlap the sides to wrap it up.

FISHCAKES

Ingredients

2 medium mealy potatoes, such as Russet,
    peeled and chopped
1 cup bread crumbs (see page 34)
1 x 5³/₄-ounce can of tuna or salmon
    (4¹/₂ ounces drained weight)
4 scallions, trimmed and finely chopped
2 tablespoons chopped flat-leaf parsley
juice of 1 lemon
all-purpose flour, for dusting
sunflower oil, for brushing
salt and pepper

MAKES 4 to 6

Serving suggestion

Serve these with a yummy homemade pea sauce.
Cook 1 cup frozen peas according to the package
directions, then transfer to a bowl. Crush lightly
with the back of a fork and mix with 3 to 4
tablespoons crème fraîche or plain yogurt.

1 Heat the oven to 325°F. Put the potatoes in a saucepan, cover with cold water, and bring to a boil. Add a good pinch of salt and cook for about 15 minutes or until soft.

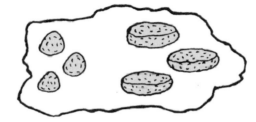

2 While the potatoes are cooking, spread the bread crumbs on a baking sheet and bake for 6 to 8 minutes, until they are golden brown.

3 Drain the potatoes and put them back into the pan. Mash, then let cool.

4 Put the tuna in a bowl and use a fork to break it up into small pieces. Stir in the scallions, parsley, lemon juice, and mashed potato until they are well mixed. Season with salt and pepper.

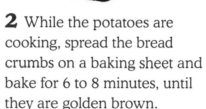

5 Sprinkle a little flour on a clean counter. Make sure your hands are clean, then lightly dust with flour. Shape the mixture into 4 to 6 balls then flatten into patties, just like a burger.

6 Roll each fishcake in dried bread crumbs (press them down to make the bread crumbs stick) then put on a plate. Cover with plastic wrap and chill for 30 minutes to firm up.

Tip

Chilling the fishcakes stops them from falling apart when you're cooking them!

7 Heat the oven again, this time to 400°F. Brush the bottom of a baking sheet with oil and place the fishcakes on top. Turn them over so they have a little oil on each side.

8 Bake for 10 to 15 minutes on one side and then turn over and put back in the oven for another 10 to 15 minutes or until the fishcakes are golden brown.

CURRY

Ingredients

1 tablespoon vegetable oil
2 chicken breasts, cut into chunks
1 red onion
1 red bell pepper
2 garlic cloves, minced
1 apple, chopped into small pieces
1 tablespoon tomato paste
2 tablespoons korma curry paste
  or 2 tablespoons mild curry powder
1 x 14-ounce can chopped tomatoes
$2/3$ cup coconut milk
$1/4$ cup raisins or golden raisins
pinch of salt
1 cup long-grain rice
2 cups spinach

TO SERVE
Flatbreads (optional, see page 20)
plain yogurt (optional)

SERVES 4

Tip

This is a great gluten-free dish, plus you can add whatever vegetables you've got on hand.

1 Heat the vegetable oil in a large shallow pan and fry the chicken for about 4 minutes, stirring with a wooden spoon, until lightly browned all over. Transfer the chicken to a bowl and set aside.

2 Add the onion, red bell pepper, and garlic to the pan and stir-fry for about 5 minutes, or until starting to soften. Add the apple and cook for another 3 minutes. Add the tomato paste and curry paste or powder and cook for 1 minute more, stirring.

3 Return the chicken pieces to the pan and add the chopped tomatoes, coconut milk, raisins, and salt. Quarter-fill the tomato can with water to rinse it out and add to the pan. Bring to a boil then turn down the heat until it is gently bubbling and cook over low heat for about 20 minutes.

4 While the curry is cooking, prepare the rice. Put the rice in a strainer and rinse it under the cold faucet.

5 Tip the rice into a heavy saucepan and cover with cold water. Bring to a boil then turn down the heat until it is gently bubbling and cook for about 10 minutes with the lid on. Take the pan off the heat and let the rice sit until the curry is ready.

6 Stir the spinach into the curry and cook for about 3 more minutes, until the spinach has wilted. Serve with the cooked rice and flatbreads if desired, with a dollop of plain yogurt on top of the sauce if desired.

Veggie variation

Replace the chicken with 1 x 14-ounce can chickpeas (drained and rinsed) and 2 sweet potatoes, peeled and cut into cubes. Leave out step 1, but add the oil at the beginning of step 2 and stir-fry the sweet potato along with the other vegetables. Add the chickpeas in step 3 instead of the browned chicken.

ICE POPS

Ingredients

(BASIC INGREDIENTS)
³/₄ cup milk or dairy-free alternative
2 to 3 teaspoons honey

STRAWBERRY MILK POPS
3 cups strawberries, hulled

BLUEBERRY POPSICLES
1 cup blueberries (fresh or frozen)
1 banana

RASPBERRY AND KIWIFRUIT POPS
1¹/₂ cup raspberries
3 kiwifruit, peeled

MAKES ABOUT 4, DEPENDING
ON SIZE OF MOLDS

1 Put the milk and honey in a blender and whiz together with your choice of fruit until smooth. Fill ice pop molds with the mixture, and freeze for at least 2 hours until solid. If you want to layer pops with two flavors, blend the fruits separately with half the quantity of milk and honey per fruit and half-fill the ice pop molds. Freeze for 1 hour then top off with the other flavor and freeze until solid.

STRAWBERRY SUNDAE

Ingredients

3 cups strawberries
strawberry or vanilla ice
  cream, or both
mini meringues or spray cream

SERVES 4

Tips

* Decorate with mini
marshmallows, chopped nuts,
or chocolate sprinkles *

* Add a layer of broken-up
meringues *

* Bananas and raspberries
taste great in sundaes too *

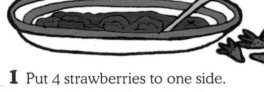

1 Put 4 strawberries to one side.
Remove the hulls from the other
strawberries and mash half in
a bowl. Slice the remainder.

2 Layer up 4 bowls or glasses
with sliced strawberries, ice
cream, and mashed strawberries.
Decorate the top with halved
strawberries and spray cream
or a mini meringue.

APPLE PIE

Ingredients

6 Granny Smith apples,
  peeled, cored, and
  thinly sliced
juice and zest of ½ lemon
⅔ cup light brown sugar,
  plus extra for sprinkling
1 teaspoon ground cinnamon
water, for brushing
milk, for glazing
1 package ready-rolled
  short-crust pastry

SERVES 6 to 8

1 Heat the oven to 400°F. In a bowl, mix the apples with the lemon juice, zest, sugar, and cinnamon.

2 Tip the filling into a pie dish. Brush water around the edge of the dish.

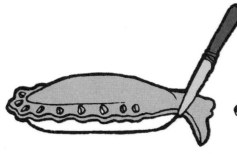

3 Carefully unroll the pastry and place over the dish. Trim the excess. Press the edges of the pastry into the dish with a fork to seal.

4 Use the pastry trimmings to make decorations for the top if desired. Make a small slit in the top so the air can escape, brush with a little milk to glaze, and sprinkle with a little sugar. Bake in the oven for 40 to 45 minutes or until the pie is golden brown and bubbling.

OATMEAL BARS

Ingredients

¹/₂ cup (1 stick) butter, plus extra for greasing

¹/₂ cup light brown sugar

2 tablespoons golden syrup, light corn syrup, or honey

2³/₄ cups rolled oats

OPTIONAL EXTRAS

¹/₂ cup mixed nuts, coarsely chopped

1 cup mixed dried fruit such as raisins, cranberries, or apricots

1¹/₂ tablespoons pumpkin or sunflower seeds

MAKES 16

1 Heat the oven to 400°F and lightly grease an 8-inch square baking pan. Put the butter, sugar, and syrup in a pan and melt gently over low heat.

2 Take the pan off the heat and stir in the oats and any other ingredients you wish to use.

3 Press the mixture down into the baking pan with the back of a metal spoon. Bake for 15 to 20 minutes until golden brown. Leave in the pan to cool before cutting into 2-inch squares (you can cut them smaller if desired).

CUPCAKES

Ingredients

½ cup (1 stick) very soft butter
⅔ cup superfine sugar
½ teaspoon vanilla extract
2 eggs
1 cup self-rising flour
2 to 3 tablespoons milk

FOR THE TOPPING
½ cup (1 stick) very soft butter
2 cups confectioners' sugar
food coloring
sprinkles, silver balls, or
    mini marshmallows,
    to decorate (optional)

MAKES 12

Tip

If you don't have an electric whisk, beat the butter and sugar together with a wooden spoon. It will just take a little longer.

1 Heat the oven to 350°F. Put a paper liner in each hole of a 12-cup muffin pan. In a large bowl, beat together the butter and sugar with an electric whisk until pale and fluffy.

2 Beat in the vanilla extract and then the eggs, one at a time.

3 Sift in the flour and add the milk. Stir until smooth.

4 Use a teaspoon to divide the batter evenly between the cases, scraping it off with a knife.

5 Bake for 15 to 20 minutes until golden brown and test with a skewer (see page 7). Leave in the pan for 5 minutes then transfer to a wire rack to cool completely.

6 While the cakes are cooling, make the topping. You can use store-bought frosting but it's very easy to make your own! In a bowl, mix the butter and confectioners' sugar together to make a buttercream. Add a few drops of food coloring.

BUTTERFLY CAKES

7 Add a tip to a pastry bag and fill with the buttercream. Pipe in swirls on the top of each cake. If you don't have a pastry bag, use a spoon to dollop an amount of buttercream onto each cake and smooth down with a knife. Then decorate with sprinkles, silver balls, or mini marshmallows if desired.

1 When the cakes are cool, use a sharp knife to cut an upside-down shallow cone shape out of the middle of each cake and cut in half.

2 Fill the hole in the cake with buttercream.

3 Place the cut-out cake bits on top, like wings.

COOKIES

Ingredients

½ cup (1 stick) unsalted
   butter, softened
¼ cup light brown sugar
¼ cup superfine sugar
1 teaspoon vanilla extract
1 egg
1¾ cups all-purpose flour
½ teaspoon baking powder
pinch of salt
¾ cup semisweet chocolate
   chips or chunks

MAKES ABOUT 24

Tip

To soften butter, take it out of
the refrigerator for at least an
hour before you need to use it,
or put in a microwavable bowl
and melt for about 20 seconds.

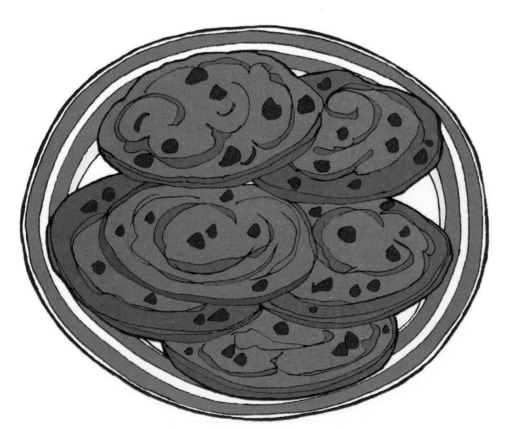

1 Put the butter and sugars into
a large bowl and beat together
with an electric whisk until the
mixture turns pale and creamy.
Still using the electric whisk, add
the vanilla extract and the egg
and mix well.

2 Sift the flour into the bowl and add the baking powder and a pinch of salt. Stir with a wooden spoon until combined. Gently stir in the chocolate chips.

Tip

If you only have one baking sheet, freeze half the dough for another time.

3 Put the bowl in the refrigerator for about 30 minutes for the dough to firm up a bit if it's very soft. Then turn on the oven to 375°F and line 2 nonstick baking sheets with parchment paper.

4 Use a teaspoon or ice cream scoop to place small balls of the dough onto the baking trays. Space them well apart so they can spread and flatten them a bit with the back of a spoon.

5 Bake for about 10 minutes in the center of the oven until they are brown at the edges and still slightly soft in the middle. They will look undercooked but will harden when cool. Leave on the baking sheet for a couple of minutes then transfer them to a wire rack.

Variations

You can use different types of chocolate and/or a mixture of fruit and nuts in these delicious cookies. Try the following:

LEMON & RASPBERRY COOKIES
Add the juice and zest of a small lemon in step 1 and replace the semisweet chocolate chips with ¾ cup raspberries, coarsely chopped. But if using frozen raspberries, don't thaw them before using!

CHOCOLATE PEANUT BUTTER COOKIES
Stir ⅛ cup peanut butter (crunchy or smooth is fine) into the cookie dough in step 2.

TRIPLE CHOCOLATE COOKIES
Replace 2 tablespoons of the flour with unsweetened cocoa powder, and use a mix of white, semisweet, and milk chocolate chips.

CHOCOLATE CRISPY TREATS

Ingredients

6 ounces milk chocolate

3 tablespoons butter

3 tablespoons golden syrup, light corn syrup, or honey

4 cups puffed rice

MAKES 12

1 Break up the chocolate into chunks and place in a glass bowl with the butter and golden syrup. Microwave on high in 10 to 15 second bursts, stirring after each burst until almost melted (it will continue to melt once you've taken it out of the microwave). Or place the bowl over, but not touching, a small pan of gently bubbling water, stirring from time to time to help it along. Be careful because the mixture will get very hot.

2 Stir in the puffed rice and mix well until it is covered with the chocolate mixture.

3 Place 12 cupcake paper liners in a muffin pan so they keep their shape. Divide the chocolate mixture between the paper liners and put in the refrigerator for at least 1 hour to set.

Tip

Decorate with mini chocolate eggs or mini marshmallows before they set.

VANILLA FUDGE

Ingredients

¹/₂ cup (1 stick) unsalted butter
1 x 14-ounce can sweetened
   condensed milk
²/₃ cup milk
2 cups packed raw brown sugar
1 teaspoon vanilla extract
pinch of sea salt
1 cup confectioners' sugar, sifted

MAKES ABOUT 56 PIECES

1 Line an 8-inch square baking pan with parchment paper. Put the butter, condensed milk, milk, and brown sugar in a large, heavy saucepan and melt over low heat, stirring until the sugar dissolves.

2 Bring to a boil then turn down the heat and simmer for 10 to 15 minutes, stirring all the time. To see if it's ready, drop a little of the mixture into a glass of ice-cold water—it should keep its shape and form a soft ball.

3 Remove from the heat. Stir in the vanilla extract and salt. Let cool for 5 minutes. Stir in the confectioners' sugar and beat for 5 to 10 minutes until it becomes very thick and less shiny.

Tip

The fudge will keep for up to 2 weeks in an airtight container or you can freeze it in large blocks.

4 Pour into the baking pan and spread it out as much as possible with the back of a spoon. Let set at room temperature for 1 to 2 hours, then cut into squares.

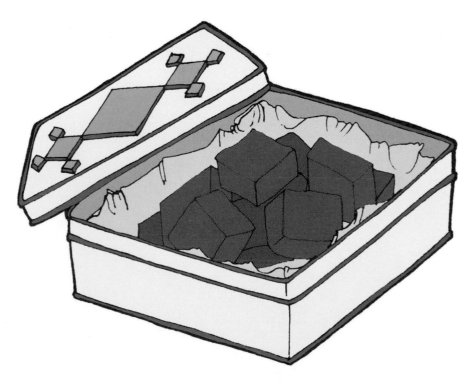

GINGERBREAD PEOPLE

Ingredients

⅓ cup (⅔ stick) unsalted butter,
  softened
½ cup packed light brown sugar
1 egg, beaten
3 tablespoons golden syrup,
  light corn syrup, or honey
2¼ cups all-purpose flour,
  sifted, plus extra
  for rolling out
1 teaspoon baking soda
2 teaspoons ground ginger
pinch of salt
2 tablespoons orange juice
writing frosting, to decorate

MAKES ABOUT 14

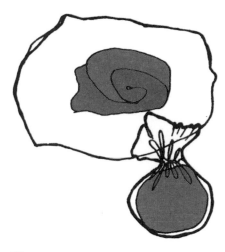

1 Beat the butter and sugar together in a bowl with a wooden spoon or whisk with an electric whisk until smooth and creamy. Stir in the beaten egg and the golden syrup.

2 Add the flour, baking soda, ginger, and salt. Stir in the orange juice a little at a time until a dough forms (you may not need all of it).

3 Turn out onto a floured counter and knead until smooth (see page 7). Cover in plastic wrap and let chill in the refrigerator for 30 minutes.

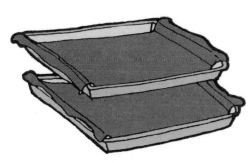

Tip

Dip the edges of cookie cutters in flour to stop them from sticking to the dough.

4 Heat the oven to 350°F. Line two baking sheets with parchment paper.

5 Roll out the dough to about ¼ inch thick on a lightly floured counter (see page 7). Cut out the gingerbread people using cutters and place on the baking sheets, leaving gaps between them so they have room to spread out.

6 Bake for 8 to 10 minutes or until golden brown. Leave on the sheet for 10 minutes to firm up, then use a palette knife or spatula to transfer them carefully to a wire rack.

7 When cool, decorate with the writing frosting.

CHOCOLATE BROWNIES

Ingredients

7 ounces semisweet chocolate
$2/3$ cup ($1\frac{1}{3}$ sticks) unsalted butter,
    plus extra for greasing
$1\frac{1}{4}$ cups superfine sugar
3 extra-large eggs
1 cup self-rising flour, sifted
pinch of salt
1 cup chopped walnuts (optional)

MAKES 16

Tip

Brownies will keep for up to 4
days in an airtight container, or
can be frozen for up to a month.

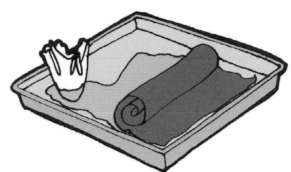

1 Break up the chocolate into small chunks and place in a glass bowl along with the butter. Microwave on high in 10 to 15 second bursts, stirring after each burst until almost melted (it will continue to melt once you've taken it out of the microwave). Or place the bowl over, but not touching, a small pan of gently bubbling water, stirring occasionally to help it along. Be careful because the mixture will get very hot.

2 Preheat the oven to 350°F. Put an 8-inch square baking pan on a piece of parchment paper and draw around it. Cut around the shape. Grease the inside of the pan and line it with the parchment paper.

3 Put the sugar and eggs into a large bowl and whisk together until well combined and foamy.

Variation

For a super-moist brownie and to reduce sugar, replace ¹/₂ cup of the sugar and one of the eggs with 9 ounces vacuum-packed cooked beets. Tip the drained beets into a blender with the melted chocolate from step 1 and whiz together until smooth, then add to the eggs in step 3.

4 Use a large metal spoon to fold the chocolate mixture into the eggs. Then gently fold in the flour, salt, and walnuts (if using).

5 Pour the batter into the baking pan and smooth the top with a palette knife, or gently shake the pan from side to side to help the mixture settle. Bake for 20 to 25 minutes until just firm in the middle. Let cool in the pan before cutting into 2-inch squares (you can cut into smaller pieces if you like).

Tip

Brownies continue to cook in the pan, so try not to overbake them. But if you do, just cover them with chocolate frosting or break up into pieces and serve in a sundae!